Farewell ... *and if Forever*

Other Works
by Johann M. Moser

Johann M. Moser

Farewell
... *and if Forever*

And Other Poems

The Diamond Ledge Press
Sandwich, New Hampshire

Contents

Farewell ... *and if Forever*

I thought to see the world
  Through your eyes.
I sought to bear your sorrows
  In my cries.

I kept my feet on pathways
  That you tread.
I wept so I could weep
  The tears you shed.

I aimed to go no farther
  Than where you went.
I claimed to have no more
  Than what you lent.

I could give you all
  I ever had to give.
I would give my life itself
  That you might live.

The Blue Boat

The blue boat is both trim and spare.
It tilts upon the sparkling sea.
Its bowsprit sports a light-blue flag.
I think the blue boat comes for me.

The blue boat has atop its deck
A silken, blue-fringed canopy.
Its tassels flutter in the breeze.
I think the blue boat comes for me.

The blue boat is a modest craft,
Its lanyards taut, its blue sails free.
Its rudder guides it to the shore.
I think the blue boat comes for me.

A Sleeping Fox

I wish I were a ruddy fox
Asleep within an earthen lair.
Wintry winds would howl outside,
And snow-dunes pile up everywhere.

I'd dream of pine trees tall and lean,
Of stony rapids fast and deep.
I'd dream of songbirds in the mist
And starlit mountains dark and steep.

I would awaken someday when
The earth gives birth to verdant spring;
When ferns sprout high and flowers bloom
When, in the woodland, robins sing.

But until then I'd tuck my head
Into my warm and furry tail,
And doze inside my sleepy den
Beneath the moonbeams chill and pale.

Medieval Opuscula

1.
Á mon seul désir

What love could such a rosette weave
Wherein our hearts as one would cleave?
Sad fortune's bane did yet bereave
A love whose loss I ever grieve.

True love is but a fleeting thing:
A glimmer on a damasked wing;
A sparkle on a jeweled ring;
A grace note in a song we sing.

I shall no longer pluck my lute.
I shall no longer tune my flute.
My days will evermore be mute,
And nights eclipsed with bitter fruit.

Yet has my plaint cause to regret
My life's most precious coronet?
Against death's dusky silhouette
Glows still my rose-girt amulet.

2.

Signum Navitatis

For then we journeyed forth—
Had that single star beguiled?
Perhaps it was a flame
Of love, heedless and wild,
That spurred our hearts to seek
That distant royal Child.

With jangling saddle bells,
And camels three abreast,
We watched that lonely star
Atop a sand dune's crest.
We treasured in our hearts
Our journey's hidden quest.

We carried in our coffers
Gold, frankincense, and myrrh,
Those talismans of life
The ancients would confer
On souls of those who died
That rebirth might occur.

We did not know whose birth
We came to see that day.
We did not know whose death
We had foreseen this way,
Or whose future sepulcher
It befell us to array.

The night was bright with stars.
The moon gleamed on a hill.
A shepherd blew his horn.
The wind was soft and chill.
Our hearts were now at rest.
The Child slept full and still.

3.

Guigemar

For Marie de France

More comely than the sons of kings
You rode forth from the castle wall
To forests where the rainbow sings
In sunny mists as torrents fall.
> *But my soul's bereft,*
> *O Guigemar,*
> *Since the day you left.*

I walk upon the ramparts high.
I watch the longships on the seas.
Dark clouds bestir the wintry sky;
The birds are mournful in the trees.
> *Blackthorns hone their spears,*
> *O Guigemar,*
> *Fountains shed their tears.*

What hearth will warm you from the snow?
What trencher serve the roasted quail?
What boding stranger's hands bestow
A leathern cup of frothing ale?
> *With what alien bread,*
> *O Guigemar,*
> *Is your table spread?*

No herds of red stags on the moor,
No long-winged herons in the air,
No springtime cuckoo's glad allure
In all the world shall be so fair—
> *As when, your soul free,*
> *O Guigemar,*
> *You come home to me.*

4.

Ballade

For Master Geoffrey Chaucer
sine qua non

As I was roaming up and down,
I saw a Lady in a gown
Who gathered flowers from a mead.
An uncouth churl upon a steed
Galloped by at furious pace
And swept her cruelly from that place.
"For me this is a wondrous thing,"
I said, invoking Heaven's King,
"How Loveliness and Honor chaste
Are seized by Lust and lawless Haste."
This Lady's fate has beckoned me
To mourn this world's sad mystery.

As I was sitting on a stone,
I saw a city all unknown
Whose gem-like steeples sparkled high.
A fiery dragon from the sky
Descended in a darkened cloud
And swathed the town in flaming shroud.
"For me this is a wondrous thing,"
I said, invoking Heaven's King,
"How earthly skill and prowess bright
Can perish in a moment's plight."
This city's fate has beckoned me
To mourn this world's sad mystery.

As I was walking in a wood,
I saw that all the earth was good:
Birds and beasts engaged in dance.
But then, engorged and eyes in trance,

A sorceress with fuming hair
Blighted all those creatures there.
"For me this is a wondrous thing,"
I said, invoking Heaven's King,
"How fecund life and freshness clear
Yield to greed of surfeit blear."
This woodland's fate has beckoned me
To mourn this world's sad mystery.

As I was standing on a hill,
I saw a throng with fortunes ill:
A noble knight in dungeon grim,
A scholar whose sole lamp was dim,
A bishop bound in threadbare cope,
A lover who had lost his hope.
"For me this is a wondrous thing,"
I said, invoking Heaven's King,
"How want and fear and bitterness
Engird our lives with deep distress."
These persons' fates have beckoned me
To mourn this world's sad mystery.

Envoi
Good King, whose Grace has no constraint,
Pay kindly heed to my complaint,
For all these sorrows beckon me
To mourn this world's sad mystery.

5.

Canso d'Amor

Vermilion-saddled destriers
Pounce and paw the dusty square;
Studded hauberks gleam afire;
Torches on dark ramparts flare.
    Yet I would tarry in her bower.
For I would be the fruit she eats.
I would be the locks she pleats.
God, what hands, what savory lips!
God, what taut and supple tips
Of orchid and of honeycomb!
Turrets of Carcassonne shall bloom
Like viols beneath a spandrel moon.
    Let the wide world see and hear,
    Unicorns consort with deer.

Shaggy hilltops' coppiced brims
Like quills of arrows, flint and tart,
Hedge the quaggy battle plains.
Harlèd heralds stand athwart.
    Yet I would linger in her loft.
For I would be the air she breathes.
I would be the braids she wreathes.
God, what long and ardent kiss!
God, what sap profuse with bliss
Of vineyards and sunflowers!
Scimitars and broadswords bare
Shall be cusped in poppies fair.
    Let the wide world see and hear,
    Unicorns consort with deer.

Mounted escorts ford the streams;
Surcoats embossed with vair and gold

Trounce and sparkle in the fray.
Visors rattle gruff and bold.
Yet I would dally in her tower.
For I would be the shift she wears,
I would be the pearls she bears.
God, what eyes in rapture meet!
God, what dulcet marguerite
Of spade in dewy spathe enclosed!
Moor and Christian as one may breed
Where wolf and wolfhound together feed.
Let the wide world see and hear,
Unicorns consort with deer.

Envoi
Valiant song, hail thee apace
To where the Rhine and Rhone embrace.
Let the wide world see and hear,
Unicorns consort with deer.

6.

Sequentia Angelorum

Indigo auroras,
Sapphire-blue;

Celestial rainbows;
Roseate dew.

Whorls of thunder,
Lightning's reign.

Leonine roar,
Dragon-bane.

Arrows of light,
Galactic spray;

Fonts of splendor,
Radiant day,

Eagles' eyes
Sleepless ever.

Tongues afire;
Flames that sever.

Abram's guests;
Israel's thorn;

Tobias's escort;
Shepherds' horn:

Astral whispers
In Mary's ear.

Sages' counsel;
Joseph's cheer;

Diamond sparks,
Pearls too bright —

Ghost-birds poised
In flightless flight.

Sun-blooms bursting.
Peerless toys:

Spanning star zones;
Divine envoys.

Moonflowers seraphic
Brisk and fleet;

Escutcheons blazing
The Paraclete.

Eternal Roses
Arrayed above.

Honor, glory—
Breathless Love.

7.

Maître Renart's
Shrovetide Confession

Confiteor, my goodly *père*,
With contrite heart I do declare
All my misdeeds, both great and small,
My lies, my theft, my sly cabal.
De Polognie à Portyngal
No greater sinner therewithal
Than I, who sought the rich to bleed
(Relieving them of excess greed),
The powerful to bring to heel
(Curbing their all too boastful zeal),
And many a good wife to enjoy
(They were neither shy nor coy.
Such things, *bon père*, could make you blush,
To your *belle maîtresse* quickly rush
By my adventures aptly spurred.
So do forget what you've just heard!)
I beg reprieve of those I've hurt:
I chomped Dame *Dinde* for dessert;
Tybert *le chat*, I cracked his pate;
Loup Isengrin, I raped his mate;
Duke *Sanglier*, his brood I ate;
Bruin, *l'ours*, I fleeced his skin;
In barnyards near I raised a din,
In barnyards far my mayhem reigned,
Rumpus, disorder unrestrained.
Goose and gander flapped and flailed;
Ducks their ducklings sore bewailed.
(What joy it was to hear them quack,
Those succulent darlings in my sack!)
Oh, how they all would hoot and sigh
As I escaped their hue and cry!

Count Écureuil I felled his trees;
Tierclin, *corbeau*, I conned his cheese.
Firepel, *leopard*, strong and lithe,
I snared and made him yowl and writhe.
Seigneur Lion, majestic king,
I stole his royal signet ring.
Chauntecleer, may he pardon me
And forgive my flagrant flattery.
(Next time I ask him home to dine
He'll trust me then and won't decline.
Though *coq au vin* will be our fare,
Steeped in that wine he'll hardly care.)
To Sire Grimbert I was unfair,
Inviting him to my distant lair,
Making his stay *chez Maupertuis*
So crude poor badger had to flee.
Blancart, *le cerf,* I scorched with fire,
His doe *Courtiose* I splotched with mire.
How many masquerades I've worn!
Abbot, bishop, monk well shorn,
Philosopher, crusader, knight,
Guildsman, peasant, anchorite;
As troubadour I roam at large,
A penny a poem is what I charge.
(The same old poem I sell anew,
The same old doggerel, tried and true.)
Certes, I'm what you want to see
(If you ignore my perjury).
All of this I've vowed to change,
All bad habits I will estrange.
Never more will I blaspheme;
Pious deeds will be my theme.
From taverns, brothels, I'll recoil
To grievous penance and hard toil.

Extortion, blackmail, forgery,
Sedition, bribes, dark calumny
Will no longer spur my stride,
No longer be my source of pride.
Alchemy will be justly spurned,
No longer swindling what you earned.
Salaciousness I will uproot,
Smudging my face with ash and soot.
With staff and badge and hooded head,
With bare and bleeding feet I'll tread
The path to holiness instead.
De Polognie à Portyngal
At palmers' shrines I'll make my call.
From life of crime I shall forbear.
When shriven pure, I shall forswear
My violent ways, my earthly lusts.
I'll live on pods and old, stale crusts.
No more *lapin* in sauces creamy;
No more *agneau* in ragouts steamy;
No more *foie gras* in clay terrines
Or partridge stuffed with herbs and beans;
No casks of sweet and mellow wine
To soothe my palate when I dine.
No crocks of ale, no *brie*, no cake.
Dear friends, now for Our Lady's sake,
Open your gates, discard your locks.
You need no longer guard your flocks,
Or hide your jewelry in your socks.
I AM A MOST REPENTANT FOX.
From you, *bon père, proficiscor,*
I venture forth to sin no more.
Cleanse me as when my life began.
(If this won't fob them, nothing can!)

8.
Sir Dismas
at the Edge of the World

With stalwart horse and armed gear
I gallop through the stormy mere.
High coastal cliffs drip o'er the shore,
Where chill winds cry and breakers roar.
Megaliths tremble by the sea.
Bleak, icy torrents, raging free,
Clash headlong with the angry tide,
As gusty snow and sleet collide.
I broach a steep, thick-crested vale
Where nothing nigh is sound or hale:
Trees droop with talismans and spoils,
With trophies rare of knightly toils:
Splintered spear shafts, stiff and cold;
Shattered sword blades, frayed and old,
Are strewn awry on mossy bank.
Hawthorn boughs entwined and dank
Enshroud a somber, gurgling stream
Where golden coins in shallows gleam.
Upon a barrow I descry
A monumental tower high:
A lonely rampart facing west,
Dread destination of my quest.
Its boar-toothed battlements impale
Cadavers twisting in the gale.
Swart ravens croak their dirges drear,
And pallid skulls on post-beams leer.
But marks of death's dire livery
Shall not deter my victory;

I will not stint or falter here,
Nor demon shun, nor foeman fear.
My sword be sharp, my shield be strong!
I'll not demur, nor tarry long.
Though sun squint shut its wounded eye
And bloodied moon stain red the sky,
Though stars abrade their wonted loops
And waves assault in thick-ranked troops,
Undaunted may my faith abide
And grace my actions truly guide.

9.

Disputatio
with a Mockingbird

Scriptor
What moves you in your mimicry
To chirp so long upon that tree?

Mimus Polyglottos
I chirp and cheep, keep chiming on
Till times and tides and tallies done
Make mock, take stock, of lissome hue,
Till tattletales and tips ring true,
Till ticking clocks and widdershins,
Tilt counterclockwise with their twins.

Scriptor
More sound than sense, it seems to me
You broadcast in your melody.

Mimus Polyglottos
Whipsaws wail and seesaws flail;
Clopping hooves and clomping hail,
Honking geese and hooting owls,
Snaffles, hobbles, clanging vowels:
Too much sense I do forswear,
Syllables sizzling everywhere.

Scriptor
I think I fail to understand.
Shall logic have no upper hand?

Mimus Polyglottos

Logic! Lobsters! Loggerheads!
Loblolly cones and trundlebeds!
What do I, don't I, have not done
To make this dazzling dander fun?
I'll trill my logic, riff my rants
In polyphonic sibilants.
My logic is in the lap of leap,
All lovely landing in a heap.

Scriptor

I guess you've clinched this argument.
Your chants are much too eloquent.
I'll hold my tongue, no longer prate
While you your raptures celebrate.

10.

"Outremer"

Crusader Song

We've ventured o'er the mid-earth sea.
Pledging our troth, our fealty.
In *Outremer* we'll meet our fate
When Jerusalem we liberate,
Or else we'll perish on the sand:
Waste deserts of the Holy Land.
The Saracen shall taste our might
Served up on shields in portions bright.

> *We have vowed what we've begun.*
> *Even if we lose, we've won.*

We fear no drums, no tocsins' gongs;
No fiery anvils' death-knell songs;
No steely sword blade's razor edge;
Nor battle-axe, nor thorny sledge;
No feathered arrows' cloven shafts
Nor sharpened maces' studded hafts.
We've bound our casques with leather thongs;
Our helmets horned with iron prongs.

> *We have vowed what we've begun.*
> *Even if we lose, we've won.*

Our mounted knights drawn in array,
Our bannered lances we display!
With spurs and rowels poised to charge,
With visors down, with tilted targe,
With battle trump's exalted cry,
We shall the paynim hordes defy.
We'll raise the doughty battle hymn,
Awaking the dormant seraphim.

> *We have vowed what we've begun.*
> *Even if we lose, we've won.*

11.

Coronet for
an Infant-King

O Master of Love's Treasury,
O let it be, O let it be.
Fashioned from every precious gem
Creation's most rare diadem.
Make it humble, slight, and mild,
Fit ornament for a Pauper Child;
Yet let it blaze with splendid things,
Emblems of sage, ancestral kings:
Burnished onyx, amethyst
In laminated whorls recessed;
Brocaded, scalloped, ivory plait
Embossed on fluted silver plate.
May platinum and sapphires true
Augment its sacerdotal hue.
Cap finials with diamonds chaste
And heart-shaped rubies interlaced;
Pearls pendulous on golden chains
And damson-tinctured porcelains;
Let faith and hope and modesty
Emblazon its fretted parquetry.
Let lapis lazuli's fine brocade
Bead old arabesques inlaid;
Let turquoise moonstones, coral blush,
Royal jade be brave and just;
Ruddy garnets, opals white,
Emeralds and jaspers bright
Refurbish topaz's sable luster,
Cusps of amber, agate's cluster.
Let ancient jewels in settings new,
Be framed by snowflakes, light and blue,

Acclaim the virtues' panoply
Engrailed around with charity.
Let what is miniature and small
Be the grandest crown of all
That shall, with its prismatic light,
Refract the sun in all its might;
Let earthly kingdoms' glory set
Before this petite coronet.
O let it be, O let it be,
O Master of Sovereign Clemency.

12.

Sir Galahad
in Brocéliande

This woodland has invited me
To set forth on this reverie
To flowered banks and silver stream
Where poppies bloom and pebbles gleam.
We roam alone, my steed and I,
Through leafy archways lush and high
Beneath great pied canopies
Of larch and oak and linden trees.
The woods about are brisk with song
Of rustling birds in sprightly throng.
Dusky shadows disport and play
In checkered sunlight on our way.
Faint elfin whispers rise and fall
From sighing winds and cascades tall,
While dragons fierce in sunken dens
Brood silently among the fens,
And griffons couchant, rampant beasts,
Embower groves of Druid priests.
Thorn-studded tendrils, looped, forlorn,
Swaddle the elusive unicorn.
We stoop to probe a forest pool
Dank and darksome, deep and cool,
Where water sprites are said to dwell
With black-webbed toes and sloe-eyes fell.
Now and then, with awe profound
We spy a green and grassy mound
Whence faery knights and ladies ride
Their white-flanked mounts with prancing stride.
Through ivy-cloistered galleries,
Past coastlands perched on sapphire seas,

By impish shrubs and wispy lights
Our journey leads through days and nights,
Drawn forth by spirits pure and fair
With jasper crowns and amber hair:
Those who succor and keep up
The Chapel of the Sacred Cup.
Passing pilgrim, bold and true,
Hear the tale I send with you:
If to Arthur's realm you stray,
When you see him deign to say
That you encountered, staunch and glad,
His faithful knight, Sir Galahad,
Who wanders these enchanted lands,
His fealty sealed with royal hands,
To bring back home to Camelot
What in these woodlands he has wrought:
No hunted game or knightly spoil
Or lays of martial skill or toil
But wisdom's ingots, crystal-bright
Sheer radiance of eternal light.

13.
Hymn of the Flowers

Macaronic verse

Bluebells, orchids, nenuphar;
Vervain, daffodil:
    Chanterai tous les jours
    Que je vivrai,
O flames of joy and my heart's ease.
What was hidden, now is found:
    L'Amor,
      La Flor,
    Qu'est de Paradis.

Larkspur, hyssop, hollyhock;
Rosa sine spina:
    Chanterai tous les jours
    Que je vivrai,
O lioness and unicorn.
What was empty, now is full.
    L'Amor,
      La Flor,
    Qu'est de Paradis.

Jasmine, day's eye, columbine,
Dandelion, cinquefoil:
    Chanterai tous les jours
    Que je vivrai,
O fount of life and my delight.
What was silent, now is said.
    L'Amor,
      La Flor,
    Qu'est de Paradis.

14.

Estampie

Stamp, stomp, leap, and hop,
Twine, twist, unloose the knot.
Bounce to right and bounce to left,
Give it lightness, give it heft.
Hoist your partner in the air,
Make her want to hover there.
  Let's be blithesome, let's be free!
  Let's dance for all eternity.

Tap with heel and tap with toe
Clogging, slogging, fast and slow.
Bluster, fluster, scold, and play.
Make all sorrows run away.
Sidle up and sidle down.
Make your kerchiefs swing around.
  Let's be blithesome, let's be free!
  Let's dance for all eternity.

Carp and caper, laugh and scream!
May joyfulness now reign supreme!
Hear the bagpipes skirl and tweet
As thumping tabors keep the beat.
Let our heart-chords twang awhile,
Our world encircled with a smile!
  Let's be blithesome, let's be free!
  Let's dance for all eternity.

Untimely Epitaphs

For a John Donne Scholar

It's odd you never deigned to ask,
Even with your dying breath,
Those questions that breathed life for him
Answered only at his death.

For the Lion in the Zoo at Kabul

I never saw a heart so spent,
A weariness so deep.
What shall those regal eyes behold
When wakened from that sleep?

For the Hummingbirds
Who Disappeared from My Feeder
September 11, 2001

In autumn of that year you fled
Across the fabled sea.
No floral song, no scented tears
Shall lure you back to me.

For an Unborn Child

I saw you dance in clover fields.
I saw you dance at night.
I saw you bind the scattered stars
In coronals of light.

For Myself

Those tomes you never opened,
Those pages never read,
Shall rejoice your heart somewhere
Long after you are dead.

The Return

Remember me home to thee,
    O Love of the Blossoming Hills!
Remember me home
    To our honeycomb, sated and rich;
To the sunlight and rain,
    To the nurture and tillage and toil
Of seasons and years;
    To vineyards pruned and primped;
To the cider-press and the wine—
    Our casks stored deep in the cellars;
To the warm and fragrant soil
    We coiled and furled and seeded:
The fallow and furrowed depths
    We nourished again and again,
Feeding, in time, what fed us,
    Breeding, in time, what bred us,
Living our lives for lives
    Of those who will live beyond us.
Our rafters were garnished
    With rosemary, sage, and thyme;
Mortar and pestle replenished
    The loaves upon our table.
For now the lilacs and rhubarb
    Summon me back to our garden gate.
Remember me home,
    O Love of the Blossoming Vales!
Remember me home to thee!

The Cuckoo's Song

I hear your song,
Lonely bird.

The woods are silent.
Your song is sad.

It echoes from afar
Across the valley.

A pine bough murmurs
Overhead.

A drizzle of sunlight
Sifts through the forest.

I listen to your song,
Lonely bird.

It is a sad song:
The woods are still.

Don't be shy, lonely bird.
Don't fly away.

Though you are far from me,
We sing together.

For Emily Dickinson

Frankly I had thought you were
Just something of a lark, a purr.
With cute and trifling slanted rhymes
Showing how your heart repined
For life, and love, and beauty rare,
Incised in verses plain and spare.
Or perhaps, as critics claimed,
You bled a spirit stumped and maimed,
Lusting (like them?) for power and fame,
Seeing what faithless hearts would see:
Contrary to all you seemed to be.
My incredulity was not enough
To stay their costs or call their bluff.
Then recognizing what was true,
I read once more, I read anew
What I had so long deferred:
Metaphysician of flower and bird,
Smithy of tropes beyond compare,
Mistress sublime of praise and prayer,
Of late I come to greet you now,
You alone of the milling crowd,
Delivered from the frauds and bores
The Donne, the Herbert, of our shores.

"Good Night, Sweet Prince"

A cat? Yes, a cat! A simple household cat;
 Felis domesticus. For you depart this day
To sleep beneath the pine boughs on the hill.
 How shall we presume to praise
Your brindled vest of brown and gray;
 Your face and feet as shimmering white
As snow upon a sunny field;
 Your black-ringed, magisterial tail?
We shall miss you,
 Lithe stair-climber, dweller in lofts,
Imbiber of new-fallen rain,
 Stalker through the lilies in the dawn.
You were our hearth-companion
 In long winter evenings by the fire—
Old wanderer, old wayfarer, old friend.
 We thank you now and ever
For the peace and solace of your ways.
 In your dreams of Paradise,
We ask you to remember our devotion.
 Good night, glad comforter of our days.
"Good night, sweet Prince."

Leucothea

ηρ 'Οδυση ελεησεν, αλωμενον, αλγε εχοντα
αιθυιη δ'εικνια ποτη ανεδυσετο λιμνησ.

She took pity on Odysseus, adrift, beset with hardships.
As a gull she arose, beating her wings, from the sea.

Odyssey, V, 336-7

Goddess of alabaster seas,
    Of iris clouds and pale sea-flare.
Goddess of the shore birds,
    With lilac arms and milky hair.
Goddess of oleander moons
    Glazing waves with silver glare:
Leucothea, white–eyed goddess,
    White-plumed pelican, fleet and yare,
Amend my grief. Attend my prayer.

Goddess of the ivory sails,
    Of bleachèd hulls and yard-arms fair;
Goddess of the conch shells,
    Of lucent domes in pearl-bright air.
Goddess of the chalky cliffs,
    Of sunny beaches blanched and bare.
Leucothea, white-veiled goddess,
    White-tailed gannet, lithe and rare,
Avert my sorrow. Attend my prayer.

Dizains

In morte et in vita

In morte

I

I sought you, hapless, hopeless, in my grief
Whose ashen loaves had been my only portion
And whose desolate cups had been my fare,
My urns devoid of salubrious wine.
How could I mend those days so sore and broken
The yield of bitter herbs, the scattered tares,
Valleys of bones, the heaps of husks and pods,
Whereon I fed, more sparse than I could spare?
I am the prey of prey upon my trail,
Where, hunter, hunted, all my spirits fail.

II

I do not think this land was meant for me:
Its barren stubble hills, its dusty plains;
Its dim pathways narrow, dank, and airless;
Its hollows flush and rank with toxic weeds.
Yet I have built my hut and sown my seed
Among these acrid streams, these briar knolls.
And I have ceased to dream of lucent shores,
Of islands lapped by far-off, sun-drenched seas.
I bend my back to break hardscrabble soil,
The task itself sole purpose of my toil.

III

Why am I obliged so often to remind
Myself that things have gone so far amiss?
They tell you to forgive, forget; to put
Aside what grievance can no longer fix.
All that is well; I'm eager to comply.
My talent for forgetfulness is prompt
To muse upon a foxglove, or a stein
Of cold, succulent beer. A peaceful niche
I would seek and find; 'til the shrill refrain
Of reproachful lips renews again my pain.

IV

Who does not think that skies will always glow
Along the seams of welcoming horizons;
That age-long mysteries shall be disclosed
And woven into dense tapestries
Whose texture and design will then ensure
Our heart's bold venture and safe arrival?
Yet I would prefer to hide and shelter
In catacombs my faint and timid faith.
For I have seen three shadows on the hill;
I have heard the cries that maim and kill.

V

The scurf, the rasp, the scrap, the gnash and yelp
Of angry years; the scars of last farewells;
All that bitter tramping in the dust;
The hurtles, brambles, lopped and limbed, absconded;
The strut, desertion, love bereft and left
To fend and stumble in the chirming squall.
What proud noblesse can possibly survive
When sentinels themselves abandon posts?
Who will gainsay, who will deny, contest,
What brassy beaks and scoffing tongues attest?

VI

Hence, we scrape together things, sundry things,
Raking them out of sand and dust and refuse,
Admiring our paltry piles, our claw-like marks
Encircling small, triumphant peaks on top.
Exercising care and rapt attention,
We make them neat and natty in their squalor.
We shake our heads in wonder as we gaze
Self-satisfied at what we've done, our prize
Won from our sordid stock of bones and rubble,
Potsherds, shattered glass and rags and stubble.

VII

It's fun to hang around in dimly lit cafés
Stroking the rim of a half-filled demitasse
Of cold *espresso*, while one smirks and gazes
Contemptuously on folks who hurry by.
It's fun to sit inside oneself like this,
Numb, in ceremonious contentment,
Savoring the sweetness of futility,
Distilling ambrosia from dire distress:
Seductive sorrow succors all one's care,
Granting reprieve in nothingness and despair.

VIII

I wear a chaplet bound upon my brows,
Base ornament, woven of tares and weeds,
Cachet of victories and vainglories won,
A sense of things now done, no more to do.
How sweet it is to draw up lists and logs,
Memoranda of projects trite and stale:
Here I drove a nail, and there I filled a pail.
Such catalogues are all I have to show.
Old albums filled with trivia I shall leave
To those who have naught else to pine and grieve.

IX

We know well, all too well, this House of Grief;
Know well its corridors, its upper rooms,
Its stairwells, porches, musty attic chambers,
Its crepe-drooped parlor where bewildered guests
We fête at times in somber robes and ribbons.
We know its floors bestrewn with broken glass,
Its mirrors cracked and darkened with the years
Reflecting what grim masks could scarce conceal.
We know the doors, the gates; we lead inside
Mourners whose stooped and groping steps we guide.

X

Wherein shall I repose my heart and reins:
In a Canopic vase of lambent alabaster
Sealed up with molten wax and amber resins
Encased in sheaths of honey fair and fine?
What funeral hoard, what tomb
Half buried in the wayward desert sands
Shall huddle me in its ancient darkness,
Perhaps too soon forsaken and forgotten?
What probing stranger shall bring back to mind
What in my sorry haste I left behind?

XI

My soul is a paddock full of shattered glass:
Of broken crystal vases, windowpanes,
Decanters, bottles, bowls, and splintered jars.
They contained me once, gave me form and place,
Measured out my portions, not so long ago,
Where now I pick my way through sharpened blades
And clear a path where I can safely go.
If I feign to relish this gaudy glaze
It does no good to palliate my lot.
I've paid with grief for all that I have got.

XII

I tried to do what I could do.
What other options did I have?
The gifts I sent were all returned,
With neither courtesy nor grace
But with anger and contempt,
As if the offerings themselves
Were poisonous and basely meant.
I have no will to contradict
Where contradiction can't avail
And truth itself can't fail to fail.

In vita

XIII

Be still, my heart, and hold your tongue.
Stay in your place, and set me free.
I have more pressing things to do
Than wallowing in your misery.
Those losses, promises unmet,
Stark disappointments, brute and sere,
Each day you love to reawake.
No misfortune will you spare.
Yet you remind me who I am,
Beneath all sanguine poise and sham.

XIV

For what I thought was lean was fat indeed;
And morsels all too sparse and crude and sallow
Were, in their very diminution, rare
And rich, and laden with a lavishness
That belied the cornucopias
I fancied in my fondest reveries,
Whereby I meted out my ends and means.
This much I know, this much I may have learned:
That what I ever grieved as void and spare
Bestowed more fullness than I have learned to bear.

XV

Hence, I am glad that what was lost was lost.
Had we won, retained, coddled, and affirmed
What we were in the vesture of our pride,
We would fester, still the same, the same as ever,
Locked, imprisoned, bound and tied, victorious
In our blindness, arrayed in caps and bells,
Strutting cocksure like a crowing fool.
For, if an angel came, it came in time
To chase us from our pokes and crack our pates
Impugning both our follies and our hates.

XVI

What can it mean that one could be beloved?
How difficult to ascertain what is
Surely our most primal expectation:
Our first and foremost impulse to be nurtured
And kept warm and safe in soft embrace.
I won't try to fathom this, not now or ever.
Can heart, soul, mind, intellect, or spirit
However you may prefer to call it,
Utter in terms most apposite and wise
What our flesh at once can recognize?

XVII

Let us not be too eager to regret
Our regrets; nor be too eager to repel
The sorrows and bereavement of our souls.
That we have had them only shows us that,
However marred our obverse coins may be,
The reverse sides, as hidden as they were,
Were but the tokens of the face of love.
I would regret if I could not regret
The dark shadow that in my heart resides
Where this, my song, my song of joy, abides.

XVIII

It is enough, is it not, just to heal:
To slumber in the sun, or by the fire;
To bask on summer beaches by cool bays
Where sea-winds softly groom the grassy dunes
And seagulls rise and dip beyond a quay?
The wounds and loot of ages need not tarry
Nor chasms gashed so deep within our bones.
Sturdy flesh will mend, restore, bit by bit,
Joints rejoined, refreshed, and will soon repair
What too frail spirits lost in their despair.

XIX

Poseurs, they said, and harlequins and clowns
Whose indolence and greed will milk you dry,
Whose subterfuge will render you inert
And vain, and buried alive in drooping pain:
This, they said, was what I chose to follow.
But I'll not paint my ragamuffin soul
In garish colors, all too motley bright;
Nor return on those who gasp in wonder
At what they see as foolishness and shame
My own reproach for what we all can claim.

XX

Go forth, feckless soul, and wend your way
Among these savage canyons steep and ragged.
Skirt needled cacti, prickly thorn grass where
Each step shall risk the wily serpents' stab,
The poison sting of scorpions in the dust,
And wings of vultures pinned against the sky.
The sun will peak, the sun will surely pale;
Praise, in the end, there is a sun at all.
And let this be, in the end, your story.
And let this be, in the end, its glory.

XXI

I'm on to "stuff" (forgive the word!) too rare,
Too fine, for—can I say?—"the likes of me."
I twist my tongue; I crudely stoop to slang,
Enjamb my lines too recklessly and curt,
Split an infinitive or two. I'm sorry.
Yes, I'm sorry. Thoughts bustle here and there,
Crowding out the common sphere; *Misery,*
Thou hast no peer. Stumble, fall, at each step—
I'll catch me at the end, I fear, and tear
Ajar the gates of splendor everywhere.

XXII

My faith is like a guttering candle
Aflame in a calamitous windstorm.
At times it dwindles to an orange nub,
A frail ember lodged in the wicker's eye.
Why it lingers on I cannot say.
Should it then not die: shriveled, ashen, cold?
But when it almost dies, it blazes up
Again, again; as if the raging storm
Was impelled to stoke its failing light:
Darkness itself spawns something clear and bright.

XXIII

White tiger, upright at my fence;
White tiger, at my gate you stand.
I lift my arm to press your paw.
You lift your paw to press my hand,
I do not know who put you there;
I do not know who put me here.
Your eyes meet mine in love and pain,
My eyes meet yours in love and fear.
White tiger, let us tear and rend;
White tiger, let us heal and mend.

XXIV

How shall I dawdle here, how be amazed
In realms of joy I never thought to enter?
The trees cast off their somber gloom, the hills,
As promised, skip like lambs and kids in play.
Stones and stars and whirling ocean streams
Join in the cosmic dance I see today.
I shall not hesitate to add my songs,
Unstitch my lids, unbind my feet from thongs.
A hawk unleashed, I'll clasp the golden skies
And make the sun stoop down to kiss my eyes.

Florida Peckerwood

Ol' peckerwood says, "Ah jus' don' git it":
Brown, unshaven, frazzled pants and shirt;
Wide-brimmed hat pushed back upon his head,
Stooped, bedraggled, hands like knotted ropes,
He squints at me and shakes his head in wonder.
Nearby the yachts are swaying at their moorings;
Crowds amble along the boardwalk
Crunching popcorn, lapping ice-cream cones;
Yellow beaches bloom with red umbrellas.
Picnics, kids, towels, blankets, pink balloons
Sprawl pell-mell beneath a tropic sun.
Café verandas hum with clientele.
Condos parade in single file along the coast:
Tall, white, and stark, like missile silos
Aimed at far-off shores across the sea.
An angler snags a shark out of the surf;
He props a chock of driftwood in its jaws.
Folks run to see. It slaps its tail; it shudders, dies,
Its thin, cold eyes affixed upon its captor.
Overhead, turkey vultures tilt and glide.
Ol' peckerwood blinks his aged lids at me.
I say back to him, "I just don't get it either."

Hazelnut

The least shall not be forgotten.

Juliana of Norwich

O Hazelnut,
    My Hazelnut.

O Acorn,
    In my Woodruff.

O Pine Burr,
    And Hemlock Cone.

O River Bloom,
    And Spangled Dome.

O Firefly
    Glittering on my Tomb.

O Snowflake
    On the cold Sea-Foam.

O Almond
    In my Honeycomb.

O Hazelnut,
    My Hazelnut.

That Thing

That thing,
    That wayward thing,
We can't recant;
    That backward thing
We can't supplant,
    That untoward thing,
That thing.

That thing,
    That awkward thing,
We can't defray;
    That froward thing
We can't gainsay—
    That coward thing,
That thing.

The Loser

Pear-shaped, hairless, short, and fat,
Pimpled visage, puckered, flat,
Hare-lipped, buck-toothed, pigeon-toes,
A pug nose that forever flows,
Sow-like ears pricked up in peaks,
A jarring voice that cracks and squeaks;
Brunt of jokes and jibes and knocks
Of curt asides and crude remarks,
I recall you from our schoolboy years,
Reduced to howls and bitter tears:
Clumsy, awkward, gauche, and dense—
The classic "loser" in every sense.
You scraped me off the road one day,
To the ER sped my way
Staunching wounds and pumping breath
Through throat and lungs both clamped with death;
Driving that ambulance like a "pro,"
Providing what care you could bestow.
In any case, you brought me through;
I owe my life and limbs to you.
If ever as "loser" you should repine
I'll acclaim you "winner" every time.

The Old Dreamer

Those youthful dreams he nurtures yet
As if each crevasse on his face
Shelters longings new and fresh;
All creases in his tattered clothes,
Every fold in his old hat
Harbors still some treasured hope,
Some aspiration he still holds dear:
Friends whom he could understand;
Friends who understood in turn;
Soft hands held in tenderness;
Smiles that ever welcomed home;
Joyous seasons of the year;
Roses blooming in a yard;
Lighted windows late at night;
Kindled hearths in winter's cold;
Cheerfulness of cup and bowl;
Kindred hearts and kindred souls;
Distant vistas, bright and bold;
Lofty things to know and think;
Familiar places, voices, faces,
Sacred enclaves, always near,
Where one could play and pray and cry,
And work and laugh and celebrate.
For if his heart was often broken,
And he must bow his head in shame,
Or if scoffers base and scornful,
Dismissed him as a witless fool,
His youthful dreams he yet sustained.

Some might not call them dreams at all
But proper ends of mind and soul:
Not vain, not aimed at empty gain,
Nor grasping for a tarnished fame;
But purposive and grand and whole—
Promising fullness in his age,
Granting solace in his pain.
Old dreamer, stooped and broken,
Old dreamer, bent, forlorn,
Though your garb is frayed and torn,
Your dreams have shown my way.

Sad Monkey

What will you do, sad monkey,
Sad monkey, peering down at me?
What will you do, so gawky and awry?
Monkey, my sad monkey, do not cry.
Braided locks are looped and frail.
Orchids' smocks are stooped and stale.
Leafy frocks are drooped and pale;
Sad monkey, yet we will prevail.
Upon your perch has fallen rain;
Some sun will sometime shine again.
The tears you shed are my tears too;
Your fears are fears I share with you.
Our sorrows we shall ever blend.
Together we'll bear them to the end.

The Horns of Elfland

O, sweet and far, from cliff and scar,
The horns of Elfland faintly blowing!

Tennyson

They summon us, those mournful horns,
To broach a woodland thick with thorns
Of blackberries and ravens' rooks,
Of shagbark larches' lurid nooks
Where fitful gold-rimmed eyelids blink
And gem-ringed fingers curl and sink.
Perched high above the paths we tread,
Desolate ridges loom overhead;
Spring mountains shed their ermine cloaks;
White-waters thunder down their slopes,
Plunging through damp forests steep
In cloven runnels sharp and deep.
A stag drinks from a river's ford,
The icy tears of winter's hoard.
Above the marshes, grim and bare,
Hovers, through fogs, a russet flare;
Rank roots of stumps contort and twist
Like venomous serpents in the mist.
Monstrous lily pads are spread
As big as islets, baleful bred,

Where giant saffron flowers bloom,
Sulfurous blossoms in the gloom.
Behold, our flaming torchlit brands
Spiral for leagues in sparkling bands,
Wind past tarns, sepulchral dunes,
By cairns and cromlechs, dens and tombs
Where splintered stakes of scorched stockades
And ruined minsters' stone arcades
Echo our battle-wagons grim,
Our creaking wheels and brazen trim.
We dismount our knot-tailed cobs
To roast viands at fiery hobs
And pour out drams of sloe-black wine
From noggins bound with golden twine.
Winds sough through woodlands plush with moss
While barques of dreams sail us across
In swan-winged fleets the wan lagoon
Beneath a sickle-bladed moon
As Zephyr churns the night-green waves
And Phosphor trims his lantern's blaze.
For who can hear those horns and fail
To muster kinfolk on the trail
Through Elfland's dim and spectral way,
Where fractious fail and faithful stay
A course where steadfast hearts will play
Among the world's rare mysteries:
Thresholds of Heaven's galaxies—
Sacred carousels in the skies,
Whirling forever before our eyes.

Ash Wednesday 1945

The blood of the land, like bronze and lead.
Sumerian Lament over the Destruction of Ur

O that my head were a River of Waters
Mine eyes a fountain of tears
That I might mourn day and night
For the slain of the daughter of my people.

THE STORM THAT KNOWS NOT THE MOTHER.

Eyes; eyes affixed to the sullen heavens;
Old men's eyes, eyes of children;
Eyes plied with fear; eyes in parks, trams;
Kyoto, Warszawa, London, Kiyev.
Black horizons rumpled in anger.

THE STORM THAT KNOWS NOT THE FATHER.

Klaxons blaring, voices shouting,
Running feet and parting glances;
Hands grasped, loosed in anguish;
Wien, Rotterdam, Leningrad, Tokyo.
Alerts wailing over the desolate city.

THE STORM THAT KNOWS NOT THE CHILD.

Drones; growl of spiky, cumbrous wings
Glassy-faced; swollen; impaled in the heavy air;
Metallic wasps trailing poisonous entrails.
Turino, Hamburg, Caen, Osaka.
Gluttonous bellies puffed with rage.

THE STORM THAT KNOWS NOT THE SISTER.

Probe of searchlights; tufts of flack.
Thud, flash of ferocious barbs;
Spires, domes blown asunder.
Napoli, München, Liverpool, Sevastopol.
Circus tents splashed with horses' blood.

THE STORM THAT KNOWS NOT THE BROTHER.

Hail of fire; volcanic gales; immense concussions;
Trees uprooted; lorries hurled across squares.
Galleries, libraries awash in flame.
Nanking, Essen, Breslau, Kobe.
Whirlwinds howling through cluttered streets.

THE STORM THAT KNOWS NOT THE WEAK.

Shattered buildings; walls collapsing.
Cellars like red-hot kilns; sewers bursting;
Shards of glass slicing through the air.
Berlin, Coventry, Beograd, Chemnitz.
Human torches flaming in the darkness.

THE STORM THAT KNOWS NOT THE STRONG.

Terror-stem; colossal; burgeoning upward.
Sprouts of soot splayed against the sky.
Dawn at midnight; eclipse at noon.
Wuppertal, Dresden, Nagasaki, Köln.
Infernal blot of sun and stars.

THE STORM THAT CAUSES THE LAND TO PERISH.

Faces, torsos melted into asphalt.
Knee-deep sludge of bone and sinew.
Arms, heads blown through doors and windows,
Limbs stuck to sides of buildings.
A lion loosed from a municipal zoo
Roams the gutted and smoldering city.
Nuremberg, Antwerp, Rouen, Hiroshima.
Mounds of children in Shrovetide garb.

THE STORM ORDERED IN HATE.

Rain. Brackish rain. Rain heavy with ashes.
Rain dripping over the valleys of the earth.
Rain thick with earlobes, teeth, hair, fingernails.
Billows of smoke choked with the bodies of infants,
Of men and women, of families and peoples.
Hibakusha with skin sliding off arms like gloves.
Fountains, rivers, ponds dammed with corpses.
Tree branches festooned with shredded flesh.
Grim retrievals gathered into the sepulchers of eternity.

THE STORM THAT DESTROYS THE
CREATURES OF HEAVEN AND EARTH.

> *"Before me shone a River of Waters;*
> *And that River nourished the Tree of Life.*
> *And the Leaves of that Tree*
> *Were for the Healing of the Nations."*

Sho'ah Umesho'ah

No time to fathom this:
To mourn, to take account.

No time for separations:
For searchlights, towers.

No time for midnight trains:
For toxic showerheads.

No time to make inquiries:
To clutch a memory.

No time when time has stopped:
When time can have no meaning.

No time when time itself
Has no before or after.

No time when even time
Has no time left at all.

Blue Oranges

Blue oranges, green cherries too
Are all I have to offer you:
Golden claws and potted birds
Jumbled in my salad words.
Blind aviators, Eskimos,
Avocadoes tripping in a row.
Pink pineapples and artichokes,
Antic games and fairy folks:
Unsubstantial things like these,
Expressions of my heart's ill ease,
I give as what you seem to need
The best my fantasy can breed
In worlds too tragic to explore
That "magic" world you so deplore,
Investing my heart's currency
From grievous pain to set you free.

Pine Hill Suite
Squam Lake, N.H.

1.
The Hill-Farm Road

Road.
Dusty road

Winding uphill
Through birch and pine.

Rain-scented.
Fiddleheads and snowdrops.

Meadows.
Old stone walls.

Horses
Feeding among the grasses.

Above us,
Sap-encrusted cones.

Blue jays
Quarrel in the boughs.

Squirrels crouch,
Paws folded as if in prayer.

Woodchucks arise,
Peer from burrows.

Rustic gates.
Antique barn and sheds.

Old white farmhouse,
High in the mountains.

Road.
Road of vestiges and tales.

Our road.
Our only road.

2.

The Cove

Sunlit cove,
　　Misty cove;
Pleated thickets,
　　Calms and deeps;
Rocky shore
　　Frog-haunted;
Heron's nest
　　Amid the reeds.
A pair of loons
　　Glide past our dock,
Solemn, poised;
　　A mother mink
Ferries her young
　　Under shady willows.
Sailboats tilt
　　On rose-tipped wings.
Dogs are barking;
　　Children laugh,
Splash and paddle
　　In sandy shallows.
A canoe, far off,
　　Aims its prow
Out to open waters,
　　To wide and windy spaces.
But not for us:
　　Our little cove
We still prefer,
　　Its close, endearing traces.

3.
The Hill

For you:
Ridgeback arc of pines,
I hone this hymn of praise.

For you:
Pelt of lynx farouche,
I celebrate your ways.

For you:
Hayfields are shaking loose
Their golden chevelures.

For you:
Daisies and wild iris
Spread aprons to the sun.

For you:
Pine-crested chaplets
The wilderness has spun.

For you:
Glacial depths
Plumb your prodigious heart.

For you:
Totemic deity,
Our wonderment endures.

For you:
I pluck a blueberry,
Globular, ripe, and tart.

4.

Inner and Outer Dwellings

At whose behest these woven days?
The hearth-slab's warm and fretted blaze;
Stacks of firewood by the door;
Boots wet and dripping on the floor;
The stockpot's fragrant simmering
With viands planted in the spring;
Damp laundry strung from wall to wall
In kitchen's warmth; the drafty hall;
Our chilly bedrooms late at night
In goose-down quilts and woolens bright.

Whose benefice has just increased
The amply garnished turkey feast
With familiar voices far and near
To seek their far-flung kinsfolk here
Where thrice-told stories yet again
Never cease to entertain;
Children's laughter, running feet,
The parents' efforts to entreat
Their sad farewells with lavish show?
Again this year will come and go.

What vintner brewed this keen bouquet
Of pungent barn this winter's day?
Through windows high the sun-shaft falls
On livestock steaming in their stalls;
The smell of hay, of rough-hewn beams,
Old cobwebs snatching sunlit gleams;
Bins filled with brindled corn and oats,
Ripe apples in their ruddy coats —

A piquant scent, distinct and fine,
An incense boundless and divine.

What sculptor's hand has carved this crest
Of snowy rooftops, sloped and dressed,
Sheathing barn and house and shed
With whorls and vales and peaks outspread?
From icy dams along the eaves
Icicles cling like bridal sleeves,
Lacy, sleek, and crystal bright
O'er frosty windows pale with light,
Blessing what dwells beneath this snow:
Those living hearts we love and know.

5.

Summer Gardens

Sunshine's glory,
Earth's bequest;
Rain clouds trailing
East to west.
Broccoli sprouting
Like groves of trees;
Eggplants, turnips,
Pods of beans and sugar peas;
Spinach so prolific
In the springtime green;
Later autumn pumpkins,
Rounded and serene.
Yellow summer squash;
Sweet peppers, green and red;
Butternuts, zucchini,
Carrots tucked deep in bed;
Cornstalks growing high,
Stalwart in a row,
Their silky silver tassels
Dangling all aglow;
Sunflowers akimbo
Eight feet tall or more;
Hills of potatoes'
Earthly hidden store.
Tomatoes held secure
In woody scaffolds steep —
Their deep ruddy globes
So plump and ripe and neat.
Brussels sprouts so high
In tiers of latticed scrolls;
Onions, chard, and lettuce;
String beans on straggly poles;

Cabbages abounding
In broad leafy nests;
Tattooed rutabagas
Sporting regal crests.
Strong hands at work
In this fecund soil;
Brimful harvest baskets
Rewarding patient toil.

6.
Lake-Ice Songs

Snowscape in moonglow:
The immense silence
Of winter mountains.

Mink-furred forests;
Lucid glare
Of frozen field and cove;

Muted barks
Of ice-sheets on the lake:
Low booms and echoes

Astir in frosty air;
Sonic auroras,
Quavering among the hills—

So sudden, ephemeral:
Like stars with mica tails
Plummeting in the sky.

7.
Farewell to Pine Hill

Swathes of snow fell on my face,
From pine trees on the hill.
They wanted me to shed their tears
When I left that hallowed place.

"Je te veux"

You are a fallow pasture
    Swaying in a summer breeze.
You are an ivory-plaited surf
    Where pelicans trace the seas.

You are a winter sky
    With cordoned stars so bright
The moon must pause to marvel
    In its nocturnal flight.

You are a lake and cove
    Whose waters are never still.
You are those piney woodlands
    You wander at your will.

You are a festive banquet,
    A gate that never closes.
You are a font of laughter
    Wherein all joy reposes.

You are my heart's desire,
    A petal in a nook;
A melody of lovely tone;
    A lily by a brook.

You are a crown of honor
    Imperishable and true.
You are everything I ever sought,
    A paradise in you.

Lost Spring

Θαρσει, θυγατηρ μου.
Tharsei, thugater mou.
Take heart, my daughter.
Matthew 9:22

This greening has not greened my heart;
Disconsolate, I stand apart.
The verdant springtime's pert rebirth
Bequeaths me but a barren earth
Where bitter winter still resides
And balmy wind no balm provides.
Blossoming boughs grant scant reprieve
To hearts that evermore would grieve:
Θυγατηρ μου, θυγατηρ μου
Your anguish is my anguish too;
Could we have faith that through such pain
We ever could take heart again?
You are my springtime's only grace:
Through your sad tears your smiling face.

Moménts Poetiques I

1.
Soul of My Soul

Enfranchise me,
 Who frees my soul.
Replenish me,
 Who makes me whole.
Embolden me,
 Who wills my will.
Sharpen me,
 Who hones my skill.
Speak for me,
 Who is my speech.
Plead for me,
 Who can beseech.
Shine for me,
 Who is my light.
Nourish me,
 Who feeds aright.
Respire for me,
 Who breathes my breath.
Expire for me,
 Who dies my death.
Ransom me,
 Who rescues ever.
Give life to me,
 Who lives forever.

2.

In Eternum

With a nod to Sir Thomas Wyatt

In eternum:
We shall bind
All loosened sheaves;
We shall retrieve
All scattered leaves;
We shall heal
Each soul that grieves:
In eternum.

In eternum:
All errant hopes
We here shall tether;
All sundry seasons
Shall be bright weather;
We shall always
Be together:
In eternum.

In eternum:
In a single love
Our hearts shall blend;
A new creation
We shall befriend;
Our festive days
Shall never end:
In eternum.

3.

Pietà

No! No! More precious countenance
I had not cherished in my arms;
More tender lips and lids than these,
Nor face more wracked with grief and harms;
Nor cheeks more branded with the thorns
Of tears and suffering and pain;
Nor eyes more mournful and distressed;
Nor brows more streaked with bloody stain;
Nor hands more punctured and constrained;
Nor cape of matted, ruddy hair
On shoulders spread so flayed and torn;
Nor neck more dangling loosely there.
Yet what burden could be more kind,
What arduous toil could be more mild
Than grieve for Him Who grieves for me,
To grieve, like this, my grieving Child?
For love, like this, is life itself
And life will go where love has gone:
This love has ever been my life—
Yes! Yes! I shall not grieve for long.

4.

Childermas

That life is but a dream the poets like to say:
An unsubstantial thing, devoid of meaning—
For those who thrive may thus presume to claim.
But how could I have known the difference?
A dream was all I ever had to know—
A mother's voice I came to recognize;
A tread and glide that rocked and cradled me;
A sacred ark that I could push and press;
A mouth in me that craved to cry aloud
For love, for nourishment, for cool, brisk air,
And light to pry apart my yet unopened eyes.
Then, suddenly, everything went blank.
Sages, poets, poseurs, fools may prattle
All they desire of dreams and nothingness.
My dream was rooted in vital bones and blood
To wake and see a real world's bloom and bud.

5.

Mount Hope

This sole hill
    Abutting coastal plains;
This sun-capped knoll
    Sculpted by winds and rains;
This crow's nest
    Peering beyond the frazzled surf;
This lone outpost
    Poised over fens and turf;
This rare sentinel
    Amid the dune-scarped sands;
This sole hope
    At the margin of our lands.

6.

Loon

Loon above the islands,
Loon above the lake,
Loon above the wilderness,
My heart is yours to take.

Loon in silent waters,
Loon in rainy weather,
Loon in icy depths below,
My heart is yours forever.

7.
Wolf Moon

Wolf Moon,
    Iris-Moon,
        Moon-Pelt ablaze with snows.
Ice-bound rivers,
    Etched in tundra,
        Pinnacles in fang-sharp rows.
Fork-tusked fiords,
    Antlered spruce,
        Frost-flanged cameos.
White bears
    White foxes,
        White whales beneath the floes.
Owl-eyed Moon,
    Fur-coifed Moon,
        Moon-Song in Aurora's glows.

8.
To a Wild Rose

Among these bourgs of broken bands,
Among these scuttled lamps,
Alone you glow,
O Rose,
O Rose like the stars above.

Among these gulches, sun-baked strands,
Among these sharded clamps,
Alone you flow,
O Rose,
O Rose like a white-winged dove.

Among these grizzled hinterlands,
Among these sodden damps,
Alone you grow,
O Rose,
O Rose of my life, my love.

9.
Abelard's Rabbit

Avec Thibault, dans le forêt

Ragged rabbit, wounded rabbit,
Panting, moaning in deadly pain,
What blow from high, what blow from low,
Has wrung from you this last refrain?
Perplexed beyond perplexity,
I lift you in my outstretched arms
And wonder who uplifts us both
And bears our lifelong dire alarms.
Can this be how we learn to love:
With blood alone we can unwind
Our souls' gnarled substance, that we know
What was apart can truly bind?
The tears of all the universe
Shall ebb and flow while tides still run;
Our old world's age-old agony
Is what both cleaves and makes us one.

Moménts Poetiques II

1.

The Hind of the Dawn

Spare tendrils, looped and lobed with dew,
Hoofprints pressed deep in spongy moss,
Lush woodlands lulled and lean and still
Ferns and willows, where you pause
To watch, and stoop, and lap the pool
As dawn-light creeps, imparts its haze
Through tinted tufts and mallows frail.
In hollyhocks and hyacinths
You graze beside this tasseled brook,
Tall ears alert and head held high,
Scenting aromas of these vales;
Round amber eyes, aglow and shy,
Long supple legs, white-bannered tail.
You roam and browse; best bloom of all,
Flower of sweetest heft and hue,
Nimble recluse of these glades,
Dawn itself within these darksome shades.

2.

The Bulls of Bashan

O that I were
Upon the hill of Basan to outroar
The hornèd herd.

Shakespeare

Many bulls have compassed me;
Strong bulls of Bashan have beset me round.

Psalm 22:12

Wild Bulls of Bashan, stout and free!
Who dares approach them, dares to see?
In chaff, in whorls, in storms of dust,
Forward pitching, leap and thrust,
Thrashing down the mountainsides,
Landslides of brawny, glossy hides,
Haunches taut and streaked with sweat,
Brindled shoulders, humped and wet;
Their nostrils panting, eyes aglow,
Blue-tongued, slavering maws below
Snorting, lowing, bellowing loud;
Horns uplifted, rapacious, proud,
They heave and shudder, bound and lunge,
Buckle, hurtle, downward plunge
Through thorn-brake, thistle, briars thick,
Through stony gulches, staunch and quick;
Hooves as sharp as hardened wedges
Punching turf like iron sledges.
Flee the valleys! Flee the glens!
Flee the vineyards, roadside dens!
Flee the groves, the village square!
For nothing will they slight or spare:
Ploughlands, pastures, seats of pleasure,

Contrivances of trade and treasure,
Flowering gardens, parkland pools,
Theaters, palaces, and schools
Perish beneath their brute stampede.
These are not herds of human breed—
Their roars are roars of nature's right,
Their strength is strength of nature's might.

Lord of Whirlwinds, Lord of Thunder,
Breach and break these herds asunder!
From Bulls of Bashan, wild and free,
Make haste, great Lord, to salvage me.

3.

Rainforest

Coffered, dripping vaults.
    Swollen crimson blooms and boughs.
Creepers, vines sweltering
    In turgid air of noonday heat;
A jaguar crouches by a pool;
    Anacondas slither in the fronds;
Studded eyes of caymans
    Cut deftly through tepid waters;
Toucans cry and shriek.
    Armorial fragments in the turf:
A mold-encrusted sword,
    A brass helmet stained and bent.
Nearby, bright orchids bloom:
    Organdy, buff, mauve, and yellow.
Overhead the sun is jealous:
    An embittered, blotted flambeau
Broods above the wetlands.
    Doldrums huddle, flash, and nod,
Affirm the dank and hooded forest,
    The jungle's dark repose—
Its littered detritus of death;
    Decay: rank, raw, and putrid;
Its chafing, churning compost,
    Talus of sprouting, burgeoning life;
Of rebirth and perpetual renewal.

4.

Am Kamin

By the fireside

Applewood and oak
    Sparkle in the hearth.
A carafe of wine
    Rests by your elbow.
Your sheen of hair,
    Your pale-blue eyes
Glitter in the blaze.
    A candelabrum's tapers
Enshrine in gold
    Your light-green dress.
Our crystal goblets
    Are radiant and bright.
Your lips, your smile;
    The rose-red vintage
You offer me:
    Whispered phrases,
Glint of eyelids,
    Fireside glow and warmth:
Redolent bouquets
    Of hearth and wine.

5.

Rosenkavalier

White-satin damasked chevalier,
With sash and gold-sheathed rapier,
Whose feathered cape enshrouds in furls
A frock inlaid with shining pearls:
You tread through portals, galleries,
Past gilded halls and balconies.
Your jeweled gloves are poised to pose
The Glory of the Silver Rose.
Bright flourishes of buoyant earth
Announce a rich, triumphant birth.
Behold the rose-girt promenade!
The choral song, the accolade!
Spousal splendor in all its pride
Whose every blessing shall betide
Nature's consortium nobly framed:
From age to age its gift acclaimed,
Endowed among the clouds above
With brimful life and joyous love.

6.

Tristan

Car qui aime moult lealment
Moult est dolenz et trepenses.
Marie de France

Tristan, would you be sad, and ever mourn
What this dark age rejects as vain and torn,
The sorry world's most sorrowful complaint
That utters its remorse without constraint?
Departure and loss and abiding pain
Have made an exile of our own domain.
Distress upon distress shall yet confound
What contempt spares not in its paltry round,
Striving more and more to file its trenchant blade
That severs what we thought could never fade,
Uprooting all we held was good and true.
In our desperation, can we but rue
What we had sought and lost, and lost again,
The promises of those gifts love would retain?
You, Tristan, in your boundless realms of grief,
Have marked the trail we tread without relief.

7.

Idyll

The forest hamlet was not so far,
I deemed.
I rose at dawn and set upon my way.
The hills were wooded, fresh, and bright.
The brooks were tremulous and gay.
Thus passed the day.

By eventide the way was lost,
It seemed.
But the stars above glowed large and bold,
The moon slept on a mountain height,
And angels sped like darts of flame
Across the chasm of the night.

Twelve Scherzos
Slightly out of Tune

1.
The Cockscomb

He strutted, fluttered, trumpeted
Like a scarlet-plumaged crane,
Yet he never thought to learn
As much, even, as her name.

2.
Crisis in the Palace

The Grand Vizier is in a dither;
The Emperor's pet flamingo
Gulped down, this morning,
The Emperor's prized goldfish.

3.
Health Report

A brandied liver, lungs in brine,
A face as flushed as old stale wine,
A pickled heart, a kneaded spine.
Otherwise, I'd say I'm fine.

4.

My Orisons

Like a horse,
Like a captive mustang,
I shred the timbers of my stall.

5.

What Else … ?

What else am I supposed to do?
Pin the sun on a mountain peak
And twirl it, like a spindle,
At my pleasure?

6.

Poetry in a Time of Civil Disorder

How can one "turn and file" a line
Without a civitas condign?

7.

Query

Why, when beset
By catastrophic grief,
Does one *still* have to:
Clip one's nails,
Take out the trash,
And balance the checkbook?

8.

Virtuoso Performance

My heart is a clumsy gymnast.
It tumbles off a balance beam
Whenever the phone begins to ring.

9.

Advice to the Unwary

For rustling in the underbrush
Chipmunks outdo a bear —
Shows how the smallest things
Can give the biggest scare.

10.

Anthem

America, O America!
Riding west on boundless plains,
Morning sun behind me,
Bach's *Art of the Fugue*
Packed firmly in my saddlebags.

11.

The Unanswerable

How can I presume
To butter my toast,
When [..........] is suffering?

12.

In a Solemn Mood

Skittish colt on slippery ice,
Foundering skiff on a sea,
Wisp of smoke in a blustery breeze
Is about the best I can say of me.

Waiting for the Night-Train

It does seem late. I shall not worry.
The night-train always runs on time.
The stationmaster dozes in his office,
Tilted backward in his chair.
A yellow bulb dangles above his head.
He doesn't know I'm here or care.
No one else waits on the platform.
I have no luggage — I won't need it there.
A forest rises high on either side;
An owl hoots now and then.
A breeze stirs branches overhead.
I sit upon a bench and watch the tracks.
I've done my work, my day is over;
It was filled with ruts and rain
And sunlight sometimes harsh to bear.
But I have left my things in order,
Said goodbye to those I've loved,
Wished well, at last, to those I didn't.
Twilight was a blessing and a burden.
I hear the locomotive whistling far away;
I'm not afraid. I'm not alone.
The night-train comes to take me home.

Where You Will Find Me

You will find me:

Where the mountain river flows;
Where the ice-bound glacier glows.

Where the panther stalks and prowls;
Where the lone wolf nightly howls.

Where minks browse on lakeside fronds;
Where moose-calves wade in upland ponds.

Where barred owls haunt the dusky glens;
Where white-tailed deer explore the fens.

Where the black bears shrug their hides;
Where the soaring eagle glides.

Where blue herons homeward fly;
Where loons extol the evening sky.

Where bright new galaxies burst asunder;
Where new worlds are born in thunder.

Where I await, to see you through,
Where I await to welcome you.

That's where you will find me.

Coda

I listened to those silent stones,
To hill-winds' high and mournful tones;
Sat by a spruce and mossy lake
To hear the lace-rimmed wavelets break;
Stood cloistered in a woodland crypt
Where long-winged shadows rose and dipped;
Trod through grasses fine and lean
And fruited orchards dense and green.
I trekked leonine desert sands,
Heeding old lays of ancient lands.
I watched high clouds above my head,
For spirits of the animate dead
Across the plains and over the sea
Have come to share their songs with me.

Where had they gone, those children's cries,
Those vibrant voices, watchful eyes;
Those joyous shouts and smiling faces,
Far-off greetings, warm embraces,
Running feet, arms holding up
The ample plate and brimful cup?
Where had they gone, those bitter tears
Shed in torrents through the years;
The shattered hopes when, bleak, forlorn,
Proud peoples toppled before a storm
And exiles were bound to alien lands?
Where had they gone, those parting hands;

Love's old complaints, the lonely sigh,
Those lips that finally said goodbye?

Those I sought in vain sought me,
My harp slung from a willow tree:
Those living things had made their call,
Making their plea to bless them all—
The birds, the beasts, the flowering fields,
The fish and all the ocean yields,
The supple galaxies that spread
Whirlwinds of stardust overhead,
Splendors of a billion twilight suns;
The past, the present, whatever comes:
The human visage, the human trace
Marking the roads I henceforth pace,
Gleaning from every darkened lea
Daylight's Kingdom true and free.

Endnotes

Pages 4–26: *Opuscula* is a Latin term for brief studies and inquiries. The poems that this series comprises are the results of such studies and are modeled on various forms, motifs, and genres of medieval literary works.

Page 9: *Canso d'Amor* is Provençal for "song of love." This poem is modeled on the Troubadour tradition.

Pages 11–12: *Sequentia* is the term used for a liturgical hymn made up of a loose sequence of couplets, sometimes added as an adornment in a sung Mass.

Pages 13–15: *Renart* is the Old French name for Master Reynard, a fictive fox who was presented as a notorious scoundrel and imposter in animal tales and legends of the Middle Ages. He was meant, of course, to embody and illustrate the human vices of the time. His Shrovetide confession here catalogues some of his many victims: *dinde* (turkeys), *chat* (cats), *loup* (wolves), *sanglier* (boar), *ours* (bears), *écureuil* (squirrels), *corbeau* (ravens), *chauntecleer* (roosters), and *cerf* (stags). *Maupertuis* is the name of Renart's chateau. *Proficiscor* is Latin for "I depart."

Pages 18–19: *Disputatio* is Latin for a formal academic debate, and *Mimus Polyglottos* is Latin for "mockingbird."

Page 20: *Outremer* is French for "beyond the sea." Crusaders used this term to denote the Near Eastern lands to which they traveled.

Page 25: *Macaronic* poems employ more than one language. Often their refrains are in the second language, as in this poem with its French *Chanterai tous les jours / Que je vivrai* ("I will sing every day while I live") and *L'Amor, La Flor, Qu'est de Paradis* ("The love, the flower of Paradise").

Page 26: *Estampie* is the French term for a boisterous medieval dance.

Page 33: *Leucothea* is Greek for "white goddess."

Page 34–42: *Dizains* are ten-line lyric poems usually with ten syllables per line and sometimes a specific rhyme scheme.

Page 43: *Peckerwood* is a derogatory slang term for a backwoodsman in the American South, used ironically here.

Page 52: *O that my head were a River of Waters . . .* is from Jeremiah 9:1. *Before me shone a River of Waters . . .* is from Revelation 22:1–2 (redacted). The lines in all caps come from the referenced ancient *Sumerian Lament*. *Hibakusha* is the name given to persons severely injured in the Hiroshima attack.

Page 55: *Sho'ah Umesho'ah* is Hebrew for "desolation of desolation," a reference to the Holocaust.

Page 66: *Je te veux* is French for "I desire you," a title appropriated from a waltz written by Eric Satie.

Page 71: *Childermas* is a variation of the Old English word for the feast of the Holy Innocents, December 28.

Page 75: *Peter Abelard* (b. 1079), a Benedictine monk and arguably the greatest Scholastic intellect of his age, was walking one evening with his servant Thibault when they heard the shrieks of a rabbit caught in a trap. Freeing the bloody and broken little creature, Abelard cradled it in his arms, where it lay briefly panting. Then, as if acknowledging the kindness Abelard had shown it, it soon snuggled close against him and died. That broke Abelard's heart and powerfully exemplified for him the universal problem of suffering in the world.

Page 80: *Am Kamin* is German for "by the fireside."

Page 81: *Rosenkavalier* is German for the *rose chevalier* or *knight of the rose*, who bears the silver rose of engagement from the bridegroom to the bride.

Page 82: *Tristan* means "sad" in French. It's also the name of a tragic hero in a number of medieval legends. In the late twelfth century, the poet Marie de France wrote one her *lais* about him, from which come the lines in the epigraph: "For he who loves most loyally is most mournful and heavy of heart."

About the Author

J ohann M. Moser was born in Cambridge, Massachusetts, in 1940. He grew up in New York City and later in New Jersey. At Dartmouth College he majored in philosophy and studied with the poet Richard Eberhart. In 1970, he received a Ph.D. in comparative literature from the Catholic University of America in Washington, D.C., where he specialized in poetics and medieval literature. From 1970 until his retirement in 2000, he taught literature and philosophy at St. Anselm College in Manchester, New Hampshire.

Moser published a volume of verse titled *Most Ancient of All Splendors* with Sophia Institute Press in 1989, as well as edited and translated for the press both an anthology of classical Nativity verse and, in collaboration with a colleague, Robert Anderson, an edition of St. Thomas Aquinas's hymns and prayers.

Although familiar with many areas of the United States and having lived several years abroad, Moser spent his early summers in the Lakes Region of central New Hampshire, where he has now resided for over half a century. In these decades, he has formed an intimate bond with northern New England, whose mountains and lakes and lively populace have been a source of inspiration for him, even as he has devoted himself to a sustained pursuit and emulation of world literature in all its dense historicity and its universal aesthetic achievements.